Within
These
Walls

Robert A. Clay

All the best!

R. Clay

Dedication

To Linda,

Once upon a time you were taller than I and as your little brother I looked up to you. Funny, here we are over forty years later and some things have not changed. True, I'm a couple inches taller than you now, but I still look up to you in many ways.

I've watched from afar as you brought two lovely daughters into the world, raised and educated them and sacrificed your life in many ways. Now, with your early parenting responsibilities behind you, you are artfully creating your own life. I've seen such tremendous growth in you and I admire the risks you've taken and the rewards you are now beginning to reap.

Our lives may have gone down different avenues at times and were not paced quite the same, but we are arriving at the same destination. Today we are closer than at anytime in our lives. So...I am proud to dedicate *Within These Walls* to you and your achievements in life.

Love,
Robert

Contents

Contents

Contents

"If you have ever fallen in love,

fallen out of love

or fallen somewhere in between

you will find yourself...

Within These Walls"

Within These Walls

You left the TV on.
I didn't mind.
It lit the room enough for me to see
your half covered body
stretched out across our bed
as I knelt down
beside you on one knee.

I moved the sheet
so you'd be warm
forsaking the beauty of my view.
You barely moved at all
and yet I knew you sensed
my love was covering you.

Within these walls
within this room
we found who we've wished to be.
We have a love built on trust
that overwhelms the two of us
and promises that our lonely hearts
will never again be seen.

Best Of Times

I don't know why I had to wait so long
to find my other half.
I certainly wasn't better prepared at this time,
looking harder or more worthy.

You, on the other hand,
had stopped looking
and believed in only yourself and God.
You were not going to let the word love
be a part of your vocabulary.

Together we are something.
What? Time has not shown us yet.
But we do believe we are on a journey
to the best of times.

Twenty One

There were pictures I should have taken
and golden fields I should have traversed
when the clouds gave way to the sun.
There were children that didn't exist,
phone calls that should have been made
and broken promises because I was young.
There was wine from an oval bottle,
beach sand to be shaken from a blanket
and my best opportunities still laid ahead.
There was daylight before my eyes closed,
intimate scenes replayed
and the jovial way I went about the life I led.
There was the sound of metal clanging
in the harbor on windy nights
as hardware beat against the metal mast.
There was the way you spoke with an accent,
gestures of affection I'd never known
and the assumption this night wasn't our last.
There were drives to the southern shore,
spinning wheels stuck in soft sand
and believing my life had just begun.
There were white caps on the open bay
illuminated by a full moon
and the invincible feeling of being twenty one.

Gift From The Past

I am conscience of my being led.
This gift is not of my own choosing.
The words I write are given
and my angels assist in all I am doing.
I believe much that today I know
I have learned in my lives before
and the lessons that I learn today
I will use in lives forever more.

The flowing of the words,
exposing just how I feel.
This must be my gift from heaven
and at times it seems almost surreal.
The releasing of my thoughts and emotions
in verse brings a smile to my face
and makes me wonder if I was an poet
in some other time or place.

Closer

How can I get closer?
How often is enough?
If I see you every evening
will it make my days less tough?
May I offer a solution
to ease my missing you?
Let's spend a weekend
within each other's view.
We can hold and cuddle.
We can kiss and touch.
We can find carnal pleasures
in the one we desire so much.
We can talk and listen
to each other's dreams and fears,
but before we know it
another Monday will appear.
And I will ask again,
How can I get closer?
How often is enough?

As We Slept

When my youth is gone I will look back
and celebrate this night.

I will remember
you approaching our bed
adorned in white linen
as my left hand flipped the covers back
as if to invite you in.
I will remember your body
sliding in next to me,
my hand pulling the covers
up to your chin,
your cold feet against my legs
and your auburn hair
on the white pillow case.

I will recall the coolness
of the tip of your nose as we kissed,
the tenderness of your skin,
all the love we made and gave,
the smell of orange blossoms
and how we fell asleep that night.

Never before had we fallen asleep
hand in hand.
Never again did we have the chance.
We did our best to hold on
to every last second
as we tried to keep our night from ending.
We knew the morning would not be for us
and when the morning came
the first rays of light
found our hands still clutching.

When my youth is gone
and they think this senile old man
is staring at nothing,
I will be staring as you approach our bed.
I will pull the covers back for you.
I will feel my left hand
holding your right hand
and we will sleep together one more night.

The Value

The softness of your hand upon my cheek
begins the touching we both desperately seek.
A desired closeness has drawn us near.
We gaze into eyes that have finally appeared.
In a second or two we will be engaged
in the language of lips, we are not afraid.
We know the moment the first kiss begins
notions of love will invade again.
The obvious questions will always be there.
Is this love or the start of another affair?
But the question that can't be ignored or dismissed,
when our lips part, what was the value of our kiss?

Basics of Life

*The things we spend most of our
lives searching for;*

*trust,
commitment,
respect,
partnership,
passion,
and love*

*are the things so basic in life
we should never have to search for them.*

The Puppeteer

I have come to the conclusion God does
indeed have a strange sense of humor.
At times I view Him as my puppeteer
and I am His tethered marionette.
With the flick of His wrist
or wiggle of His finger my life changes.

God offers a taste of success to motivate me,
He lets me experience hard days
before the soft nights,
I live sadness before I discover happiness
and the minuses in life
always come before the pluses.
God lets me strive for achievement
and just when I think I have failed,
I succeed.
He offers me years of good health
while slowly showing me signs
of my physical demise.

He gives the earth rotation creating life,
but never allows me to enjoy
the pinnacle of each season for very long.

My favorite moments vanish quickly
as winter's new snow,
spring's fragrant blooms,
summer's balmy breezes
and fall's colorful cornucopia
are only a blink before they are yesterday.

Yes, God does indeed have
a strange sense of humor.
He gives me a heart
that is bursting with love to be shared,
a mind that dreams of being with only one
and the ability to translate
emotional personal thoughts into words.
And just when I think God
has left my love destiny unfulfilled
He awakens my optimism
with a tug of His puppeteer strings
exciting this marionette's trust in tomorrow
and introduces you into my life.

Unspoken Word

It's the unspoken word
that does the most harm
when the syllables of love that go unsaid.
It's the quiet moments
until a thought is expressed
and the distance between words
when the truth is read.
If you wonder how you got where you are?
If you can't figure out what went wrong?
Think back to the silence of your heart.
Remember your words held captive for so long.
In time another love will pass your way.
One more chance to say what you fear.
Express your words of endearment
before another love is no longer near.

No Harm

I wish you no harm.
I know the risk of loving.
I understand the danger
of exposing an open heart.
When you fall faster than another,
deeper than you should
and finally lose control of your common sense.
I know it's hard to ignore your heart's desire.
We all are guilty of loving love,
but accept this lesson and warning.
"I don't want anyone
in this relationship to be hurt,"
simply means you are not the one in control.
I surrender my compassion during our days
and always believe in my heart
I wish you no harm.

You Block the Sun

You block the sun
and there is a halo of light around you.
You kiss me upside down
and I feel your nose on my chin.
Your hair tickles my face
and you brush it with the wind.
You smile when our lips part
and it is easy to see your devotion.

I don't know where you came from.
I would have been there long ago if I did.
Did you come from a prayer
I thought was lost?
Did you know I've been waiting for so long?

Your eyes are so alive and eager.
Your feelings for me are on constant display.
I wait as you come closer for another kiss.
I see your halo of light as...
you block the sun.

There Are Dreams

There are dreams that float above the earth
beyond the dreamers grasp.
There are dreams that we live to see
though at times they disappear too fast.
With widened vision and broadened hope
we dream for we must believe
in time our dreams will materialize
and we'll live the dreams we've conceived.
There are uncontrolled dreams we recall
when we awake in the middle of our sleep,
but the dreams that we love the best
are the dreams we're allowed to live and keep.

Trying To Get By

She stayed with him longer than imagined.
He knew his life had become a total lie.
Her concern was caring for their children
now that they both were trying to get by.

She resented his late night hours.
He said, "I'm working a job I have
always despised."
After all their dreams had vanished
they did what they could to get by.

Maybe she never loved him
the way her mother told her,
"You'll recognize?"
Maybe he jumped into marriage too quickly
as he searched for what was missing inside?

Indiscretions were numerous.
Affairs released the desires they tried to hide.
Their passion was found
in the arms of strangers
as they emotionally struggled to survive.

In the future their children may hold judgement
on how the parents did not realize
a need might have gone unnoticed
while the parents were trying to get by.

There should be no blame placed in a life
when choices are so difficult to decide.
We all feel we are doing the best we can
and we are all only trying to get by.

Who's to say when the children are grown
and are given their own family to preside
if the next generation won't question their choices,
after all, they too will be trying to get by?

How We Survive

We're continually falling in love
with each other.
To survive it's something
we both need to do.
We're so different from when we first met.
I've grown and I've watched
as you've grown too.

If we loved only the person
we originally knew
and never fell in love again
as we have grown,
we would drift apart and eventually lose
our connection to the
wonderful life we have known.

We're continually falling in love
with each other
and we're so thankful
every time we rediscover
new sides to the one
we've fallen for repeatedly
who we know as our best friend
and splendid lover.

Nurture Our Future

For one of the few times in my life
I'm having trouble
holding my head high.
I'm genuinely wounded.

Ominous clouds approaching
can only be avoided for so long
before turbulent winds rip and shred
blessed peace and silence.

Come, sit next to me,
hold my body,
nurture our future
and together we will find
tomorrow's sunlight.

Night Time

My eyes have never been open
as wide during the night.
My mind has never been as active.
I never thought I'd stare
at my ceiling for so long,
but I've never longed for you before.

My ceiling fan's blade cuts through the night.
I feel the pain.
The blue glow of the moon outside my
window reflects the tone of my soul.
A small crack on the wall,
the faint normally unheard sounds of night,
and the ever present pounding of a lonely heart
looms large as time slowly moves on.

As I turn my head once again to see the clock
I find the hands have not moved.
Hours have seemingly passed within my mind.
Seconds have passed within reality.
What has happened to the ticks of my clock?
There seemed to have been so many
and yet virtually no time has passed
except for our time together.

On Second Thought

It's 5:35 PM.
She's gone by now.
A phone call would have been considerate.
An appreciative word to officially end
our affair would have been nice.

I didn't ask her to call,
but our actions made me believe she would.
I guess it never crossed her mind.
On second thought...
I guess I never crossed her mind.

Reruns

Starting over is never easy
and once again she finds herself asking,
"How many times, how many
desperate times?"

As the checkout line slowly moved
she juggled her future in her arms.
A white plastic basket will serve as a hamper,
one set of generic towels will get her by
and her basic beige sheets will be
the only thing next to her skin tonight.
As she reviews her past relationship
she mumbles,
"This new hair dryer is just like his words."

Her prized looks would never let her down.
She always had so much hope.
Time surely was still on her side.
Each relationship just wasn't right.
It was always him, it was never her.
One more savior that didn't resurrect her life.

Now she's feeling the pressure
of too many one night stands and the
broken promises that came with lust.

Her new apartment isn't new,
and when she comes home
no one will greet her.
The simplest home cooked meals,
reruns of "Roseanne"
and a glass of wine on a balcony
awaits her each evening.

Is this another beginning
or where she will end?

Her Statement

She spoke from her soul when she said,
"In darkness only loneliness can be seen
and my vision has become quite good.
I've looked for my heart and only
found the emptiness from my past.
I've waited for time and healing
and now you have come along
bringing your slow, confident,
understanding, seductive
and romantic way.
I've never asked for anything.
My simple life always seemed like enough.
Now, I ask of you in a
breath filled whisper…
don't leave me tonight,
tomorrow night or next week.
Don't ever leave me…stay ."

Your Perfume

Once…this was all I asked for.
To feel your arms around my shoulders
as my hands were cupping your waist.
Your constant breath on my neck
as my lips touched your forehead.
Swaying slowly, but not dancing
as a piano played softly in the distance.

Your perfume…oh, your perfume.
Your infectious laugh.
My affectionate whisper
as your kiss finds my cheek.
I need to hold you tighter.
I cannot get close enough.
There is no space between us.

Alone…have I ever felt alone?
With you all loneliness is forgotten.
My lost passion has been recaptured
as I open myself to all you offer.
If our night ever ends
I will leave forever knowing
the meaning of the word "us".

More Than Myself

I've waited for you,
but feared your arrival.
Without announcement,
I knew I needed to love you.
Would I be able to totally indulge myself?
Would I let myself be totally loved by you?

You're the answer
to the question I've ignored.
You're the resolve to many loose ends.
You break through my vulnerability.
You tempt me with nights I cannot forget.

If I could speak the language of my heart
the words fear and love
would not co-exist in a sentence.
Adoring descriptive adjectives
would flow through my lips
and for the first time in my life
I would know how it feels to love
someone more than I love myself.

You've Turned My Head

It's nice to know
there is still someone that turns my head.
Someone that makes me stop in my tracks
and notice the complex simplicity
of a gorgeous woman.
Someone who alerts my senses and allows
me to feel the excitement
I have not felt for so long.
Someone who is nothing more
than a dream at this point,
just a stranger walking by.
Eye contact is made and a smile is given.
"Simply delightful,"
I say under my breath as I realize...
you've turned my head.

Monet Moment

Green lilies float on darker green lake water.
Peacefully they await another new day.
Their pink flowers are the center of this Universe.
"A Monet moment," I incessantly say.

The mallards are brush stokes on the surface.
Their elegance will not be denied.
Reflections of their beauty float before them
as webbed feet paddle in rhythmic stride.

I am an intruder in their private moment
as I walk beside the lake in morning dew.
This second is mentally saved on canvas
as I garner all from this watercolor view.

In a moment light will overtake the dawn
and soft tones will become brilliant around the lake.
The sun will again repaint the sky
and others will begin to awake.

By then, I will be back in my cabin
remembering how this new day began.
Knowing I've gazed through the eyes of Monet
and visually painted with his brush in my hand.

My Child's Voice

I will always hear my child's voice saying,
"Spin me around till you see my hair
floating like silk through the breeze.
Hold me higher than I have grown
and protect me from the dangers I've not yet seen.
Lower me slowly when the twirling stops
and my feet return to the ground.
And when the spinning ends explain to me
why my head continues to go 'round.
Teach me about all the things
that don't make sense to me
and give me a kiss in the evening
each night as I prepare to sleep.
Leave the light on and the door cracked
and please check under my bed
so I'm safe from the boogie man
as I lay down my sleepy head.
And most of all when the morning comes
I hope your face is the first I see
and you'll spin me around till you see my hair
floating like silk in the breeze."

The Confluence

I watched the confluence of two souls
from my park bench. It was a beautiful sight.

Maybe it was his smile as he approached her
or the way he used his hand to curl
wind blown red hair behind her ear.
I couldn't help but stare as she flipped
his camel hair coat lapel around his neck.
She adjusted it so precisely
to repel the fall breeze.
Maybe it was the way he cupped her chin
with his fingers as their lips merged
or her body language accepting
him without reservation.
Perhaps it was the confidence
with which he put his arm around her waist
and guided her past my voyeuristic view.

On this fall afternoon
I was not expecting to see love.
I was seeking the colored leaves
that fly through the air,
the last gasp of warmth in the fall breeze
and hoping the sun would find an opening
and shine on me once more.

Instead of fall I saw love
and I was mesmerized.
I internalized their movement
and recognized my void.
Oh, to be there and know
the ease of their affection.
To walk along the leaf covered path
with such conviction.

When I journey into love again
it will be with the guidance from God
and my frail human heart.
I will fill the void left wide open
by my past hopes and dreams.
I will fly through the breeze
like fallen leaves dancing on the wind
and land gracefully upon you.
I will float in a slow and steady motion
toward my love destination
giving everything I have
while asking nothing of you.
I will curl your hair behind your ear,
cup your chin with my fingers
and allow you to pamper
and protect me from autumn winds.
I will walk with you
with my strong arm around your waist
as I watch the confluence
of our once lonely souls.

The Boundary

The red velvet rope.
The double yellow line.
The darkness we fear
approaching the end of our time.
The door that remains locked.
The corridor that guides.
The white glove in our face
saying, "entry denied."
The shake of the head
that means don't proceed.
The red traffic light that stops or impedes.
The key that doesn't fit.
The guard that we can't pass.
The legal paperwork we continue to amass.
These boundaries we face
every day of our lives
will be broken and crossed
when we finally decide
to unlock the barriers
and choose to overcome
the boundaries that retain us
from the truth and freedom.
But more damaging than a guard,
gate or a blinking stop sign
is the boundary we create
when we refuse to open our mind.

Unnatural Occurrence

I love it when the sun is out
and it softly rains.
Like tears that fall during laughter,
it seems like an unnatural occurrence.
I like to throw my head back
and open my mouth,
watch the sun filled raindrops
end their voyage on my face
and land on my outwardly stretched tongue.
I love the small drops that tickle my skin
and make my eyes blink with protection.
I love the accumulation
of rain rolling down my cheek
forming drops that remind me of past tears.
My light brown hair
becomes dark with moisture
as I embrace every raindrop
when the sun is out and it softly rains.

Jacquard Sheets

You softly sing when the morning sun arrives,
melodies you heard while sleep hypnotized.
Your voice sounds rather Celtic
echoing through the halls.
Like old-world hymns forgotten,
then suddenly recalled.
I am still in our bed listening to your tone.
From my pillow I see a picture by our phone.
It's there upon the nightstand
right next to our bed.
We're happy in a copper frame
trimmed with tarnished lead.
The notes you sing become a haunting melody
as they drive me deep into a sea of tranquility.
A painting of red rocks,
a wicker basket on the floor
are blended with your voice
to create a morning I adore.
I'll stay in our bed
and under jacquard sheets that hide
me from the world
as I await your body next to my side.
Your voice will precede your footsteps
and when I see your face
our kisses will silence your singing
and tender love we'll make.

Flirtatious

I feel your eyes staring at me.
You look away when I return the glance.
Your eyes look my way again,
but only when you feel it's safe to chance.
You moisten your lips with your tongue
and twirl your fingers in golden hair.
Your attitude is so flirtatious
as you sit posing in your red leather chair.

You try to attract my attention
with the movements that you make.
Your choreographed moves are so feminine
and exude all the sensuality I can take.
And finally when our game ends
and you think I was captured without a clue,
I offer a smile and in my flirtatious way
I let you know I was pursuing you.

The Bridge

My first thoughts of love as a youngster
came while skating around my basement floor.
The childish games played were accompanied
by the music on records I adored.
"The Wheel of Fortune" was sung by
Kay Star as I began to see
how a voice with meaningful lyrics
could build my bridge to the feelings inside me.

A small transistor radio was by my bed
early on a Saturday morning
the first time I heard rock and roll
and became hooked without warning.
I heard Lesley Gore crying at her party
and something about "Love Potion Number Nine."
By the time the sixties were over
I was singing every note and knew every line.

The seventies brought an avalanche of songs
and I continue to go back and listen.
I found Jackson Browne's "The Pretender"
and Dan Fogelberg's "Nether Land"
near religious experiences that made me surrender.
I fell into each and every word they sang
as their lyrics began to build my emotional bridge.

I listened to their notes, their music,
but within their lyrics was where I lived.

I was married in the eighties with
Rachmaninoff softly in the background.
"Rhapsody On A Theme Of Paganini" played
as I stood in my coat across from her in a gown.
No lyrics were sung that day,
just long notes that made me hold my breath
until each one had ended and the swelling
was controllable deep within my chest.

In the nineties I began to write my poetry
to record, a thought or a special moment.
I started to think back to my influences
and why I developed this talent.
I found the answer was the music I have known
through loving days and lonely nights.
The melodies and lyrics became the vehicle
that drove me over the bridge
to split-seconds in life of which I write.

My poetry today is a bridge to a time
that for many has long ago passed
and it allows those who read my words to relive

a feeling that was fleeting and didn't last.
And just like those old love songs explained
exactly how we felt
but didn't know how to reveal,
my words weave a bridge to yesterday and
the past feelings and emotions we've concealed.

A Loss For...

The angels came today and took him.
These are the words
I used to describe the loss...

.

.

.

.

.

.

.

.

.

.

.

.

.

.

.

.

there were not today and there will never be
words to describe the loss.
At least not until the angels come for me.

Phone Numbers

A home phone number
written on a business card.
A number and a private note
on the back of a receipt.
A first name and number
inside a book of matches
and one on a wedding napkin
I thought I'd surely keep.
I guess they didn't mean as much
when the night ended
and the people were out of sight.
Most numbers ended up
in the wind behind my car,
ripped and tossed out my window
and into the night.
In my rear view mirror they danced
like snowflakes on a January breeze.
With a flick of my wrist
the phone numbers were gone
of those I'd met
but never intended to again see.

Linger

When we say good-bye
I am reminded
of late evening's purple sky
as night closes in
on the last light
of the lingering day.
When you turn to go
I take one step in your direction,
inhale air where you stood,
search for your perfume
and hope to find
it lingering in your wake.
Each time we part
there's always a void
that makes little sense
and causes me to think of how,
though you leave me,
part of you always lingers.
With you and then without you,
the void is greater through time.
When we're apart I savor
what I am left with.
When we say good-bye I am reminded
how you continue to linger.

Cedar Key

Sunday morning and we were finally alone
with only the needs and cares of lovers.
Called from our bed
when the light through the blinds dimmed
and thunder's voice beckoned
for us to remove the covers.
We exited our cocoon
to take a mental snapshot
from the wooden gray porch
surrounded by the cold front's rain.
We watched as dark clouds brought droplets
to the island and the dry sand that remained.
We sat huddled together under old blankets
on the wooden swing and asked,
"Where have you been?"
We kissed and cuddled
and exchanged smiles
every time we were sprayed
by the rain in the wind.
And as the storm passed
over our fishing village
and a natural calmness returned to the sea
we promised to return
and linger a little longer next time
we visit our retreat of Cedar Key.

Déjà vu

The alignment of the stars must be perfect
and the forces of nature are in balance.
A growing harmony is around me
and the master is leaving nothing to chance.
A full moon is rising over the horizon
and a burnished sun has not completely set.
I don't understand how this will sift together,
but I think I'm approaching something I'll never forget.
I'm feeling a little bit like a perplexed foreigner
reading the language on the dinner menu.
I find a word or two that look familiar
every time I experience a little déjà vu.
There's no cause for alarm or resistance and intuitively
I know floating is how I'll pursue.
With arms stretched out and head tilted back
I'll float into tomorrow through déjà vu.

Colors In My Mind

The colors in my mind do exist.
I found them on a winding road
ascending to clear blue sky.
Golden tones complimented
by dividing lines on asphalt.
A yellow curve in the road
that implores me to continue through
rich jeweled colors
not seen since the days of my youth.
Fall leaves penetrate
and force my eyes into the forest.
I am summoned to gaze deeper and deeper.
I find myself unable
to take in the depth of the colors.
Is it gold, yellow, burgundy, or russet
that I will choose to admire most?
Autumn has given her all this year.
Every tree, every leaf is beautifully displayed.
A perfect visual gift to all as I realize,
the colors in my mind do exist.

Inner Circle

As children
we run to catch-up with the others.
As lovers our wish is not to be alone.
When we trust the people that are closest
we find comfort like we've never known.
We're connected by a single common thread
in a world that's constantly in a swirl.
Our chosen few are the friends we call family
that complete the inner circle.

Extending our arms to embrace one another.
Support given when we're most in need.
Our inner circle of friends understand
when we're injured true friends also bleed.
These are the people we have chosen to share
the important moments that we'll spend.
Our guard is down, because there is no need.
The inner circle's trust will never bend.

Selfishness

So many people beg and plead
for a change or a new direction.
They insist on another road,
a better life given without question.
And it seems I at times
are just as guilty as they.
We single out ourselves and
too often we're selfish when we pray.

Dare I Say

Do I breathe too deeply in your presence?
Does my beaming smile give me away?
Do I say "yes" a little too quickly
when you ask if I'd like to stay?

Is it possible to forever love
as deeply as when it all begins?
Dare I say we are embarking
on a love journey that will never end?

The Dance

The first time I saw her
she had a swizzle stick in her hand
and she was swirling the liquor
within her drink
like a waterspout over sand.
Her elbows were on the bar
as she stared across the room
and as I got a little closer
I saw her look of gloom.
She didn't seem to notice
when I took the seat next to her.
Her eyes were fixed straight ahead,
her side vision was a blur.
I could see her twenty on the bar
still waiting to be spent
and a lighter with a stock car's number
next to imported cigarettes.

Dewars on the rocks I ordered,
but I never made a sound.
I ordered with a nod
and the bartender brought me a round.
I brushed against her arm
as I reached for my cash,
but she never even blinked,
not even a flicker of her lash.

I settled back into my chair
to look over the room,
to inspect the prospects
and possibilities that loomed.
A blonde over there,
a brunette that wasn't too bad I thought,
but who was this lady next to me
so intent and obviously lost?

There must have been fifteen
or maybe twenty minutes that passed
before I finally spoke to her
and for a slow dance I asked.
No sooner had the words left my lips
when she slowly turned my way
and my eyes saw the reason
for the anguish she displayed.
There on her left hand, third finger from the right
was the source of her misery
and sadness of her plight.
Pale skin glowed fluorescent
around the finger that was tan
and left a sad impression
where she once wore her wedding band.

She said, "You are a stranger,
and before I tell you what I'll choose
I'll tell you I know it's my body you want
up close and against you.
I know you want to slow dance
to hold me and see just how I'll feel,
and though I'm on my way to drunk
I still know that's your deal."

I started to grin
and then I realized what she had said,
so I reached across to touch the hand
held on the day she was wed.
I let my fingers blend with hers
as our skin touched for the first time
and then I order another Dewars
as I stumbled for a line.

She pulled her hand away
and stared at me for a while
and I saw her lips begin to form
a smirking kind of smile.
Again she began to speak,
but now I could detect the slur
brought on by all the liquor
I had watched her frantically stir.

She told me quite bluntly,
"Look, I came to be alone tonight to drown
the memory of that bastard
and the truth that I have found.
I'm not here for your entertainment
or for that matter mine,
but if you wish to sit and talk
I guess that will be just fine."

I glanced around the bar
and my eyes looked for easier prey
and I wondered if I should leave
while there was a chance to walk away.
Just as I was about to depart
the seat I had occupied
I noticed as she took a drink
a tiny tear fell from her eye.

"Yes, I am a stranger," I softly said,
"but I am wise for my years
and though it would be easy to leave you
I recognized your tear.
It looked so familiar
and it doesn't seem so long ago
that my tears were falling
from a love that ceased to grow."

She turned in her seat to
face a friend that was new found
as I nodded once again
for the bartender to bring us one more round.
And then she sounded like another,
her tone of voice had suddenly changed.
She smiled at me warmly
and I was glad I had remained.
She reached across and put her hand
upon my lonely arm
and started to caress me
and offer shelter from my storms.
She asked me, "How did you make it
through the darkest of times
and what kept you going
when you thought you'd lost your mind?"

I said, "I first have to tell you
it seems to have been an eternity
since I felt stimulation
simply by the way someone touched me.
I can feel each finger of your hand
as it slides on my skin
and even the lightest of your touch
gives me a glow deep within.

But to answer your questions
before I go on about your touch,
I don't know how I made it,
I guess some of it was just luck.
I know I've always believed
the day would finally arrive
when I would again feel the touch
that would renew my love inside."

Her smile became broad
and with her touch I felt empowered,
so I asked her if she wanted a drink
before the closing hour.
"No," she said, "a drink is not what I need,
at least not at this moment.
I need for you to hold your body
against mine until we both relent.
I need to know if love can be real
or if it's always just a fake
and is it possible we could meet
on a night I had nothing to forsake?
But most of all I need the answer
to the question you earlier dared to chance,
would you like to hold me tightly,
would you care to slow dance?"

Still Something

A splinter of red became the horizon
and a gray ribbon of road still lay ahead.
The sound of our voices pierced the silence
as we searched for sanity in the words said.
What is it that makes us believe
a raised voice carries much more truth?
Why do we see things clearer
when there is a possibility we might lose?
What would one more screaming note
or firm explanation solve or incite?
At five AM on the highway to nowhere
each of us insisted we were right.
You sat a million miles away from me
as you stared into the remaining night.
Your facial reflection I found in the window
each time we went under a streetlight.
As the darkness faded
and sunlight and reason gave way to a truce.
You gave and I gave in too
and hardened positions were finally cut loose.
But is it possible a winner could emerge
from the ugliness and hurt we displayed?
No, there would only be losers
hoping there was still something to be saved.

Crossing The Line

There is a price to be paid
when the thin line is crossed,
when honesty exists only within the mind
and simple reason is not within reach.
There is damage to be done
from wanting something too much
or trying to control
what you have no control over.

There is love to be lost
when those who are loved
proceed with caution
as strengths become weaknesses
and words become misunderstandings.
There is a price to be paid
when fluid open conversations
begin to slow to a steady contained drip
after the thin line has been crossed.

Tobermory, Ontario

I will see Tobermory when the
winter winds are blowing.
I will walk her docks
and watch as tugs motor into Lake Huron.
The "Dykker Lass" will sit
tied to her stable metal cleat
and the "Dawnlight's" rope
will drape into Little Tub Harbor.

I will see Tobermory's stratus blue sky
blanket neighboring townships,
but the sky will be the bluest above her.
Marine colored waves will cup
as they approach the jagged rocks
and the marble tone chiseled shore
isn't why I came here, but it's how I feel.

I will see clusters of red leaves,
a prelude to fall's coming symphony,
flaming water reaching toward the
Grandview Hotel as the sun finds
Huron's horizon
and velvet smooth Merlot
will slide off my lips and into my soul
as I raise my glass and toast the end
of one of Tobermory's days.

I will feel her breeze separate my hair
and saturate my thoughts,
I will hike to the lighthouse again
to pay respect to durability,
and sit by the harbor and contemplate
only my surroundings.
I will be amazed how Tobermory
has such an effect on my perspective.

I will see Tobermory
when the winter winds are blowing
and nature changes everything about her,
but her name.
Tobermory will be frozen in my memory
as I found her this fall day.
Not even the coldest of winter's wind
can change the way I recall Tobermory.

The Three Cent Stamp

A letter would come to the door.
The written words of a relative or friend.
Enclosed was the satisfaction of knowing
the endorser had taken the time to spend
a moment to write down their thoughts
and offer their feelings and views.
Sometimes it was knowledge given
or details about the family news.

In those younger years
when the personal letter was sent,
it would arrive with a stamp
costing only three cents.
We would read on the back
of each ink smeared envelope
who the letter was from,
giving us excitement and hope.

We devoured every line
and occasionally would try to decide,
was that a misspelled word
or was the writing ill inscribed?
We would read between the lines
until their intention was understood.
Our eyes would swell with emotion
as we learned of family sadness and good.

In the past the hand written letter
was the best way to communicate.
Today we have become so impatient
and choose to no longer wait.
We resort to phone calls,
e-mails and faxes to keep in touch.
While the art of the hand written letter
is the communication that explains so much.

The Passing of June

Sloping green lawn.
A narrow trail leads the way.
My destination is not far
along this path of white rock and clay.
At the end of the stone
where their hectic world ends,
I find my Mecca, the dock on this lake
is where my world begins.

My bare feet skim the water
as I dangle them like a child.
And if I time it just right
I'll watch the sunset in a while.
The sun glows over the ridge
as it drops through the trees.
Signaling another June day

is passing through the leaves.

When I sit on my dock
the answers come one at a time
to all those questions
as I search for reasons to rhymes.
I collect my thoughts
and blend in my surroundings.
I'm seduced by nature
and it provides a natural healing.

As the darkness descends
and the shadows of day disappear
I lay back on my dock
as the color of dusk draws near.
I look straight up at the sky
and I find a crescent moon.
It illuminates my face
and another day passes in June.

The Least I Can Do

Confessions of the heart
leading us to different mornings
won't remove the fondest part
that made you so endearing.
The softer side in you I found
before revealed destinations
will always be around
when I think of our relations.
Once you requested to sit
by my fireplace bathing in it's glow,
in friendship I offer you a flame still lit
to talk over troubles
we've both come to know.
And if you ever feel you're alone
and you need someone to talk you through
I'm still someone who will answer the phone,
my friend, it's the least I can do.

Confrontation

Our verbal confrontation
has vicious words directed at my heart.
You tried to evoke a response from me
and you hoped that I'd take part
in your little war of the words
where no happiness lies within.
The hurtful game you choose to play has losers,
but no one ultimately wins.

There are many ways I could cut you down
and make you feel the same as you've made me,
but I will not respond with hatred
or violently abuse you verbally.
I won't waste my time or energy
on cunning or cruel words I could say
and if it's all the same to you my friend
this is a verbal game I'll choose to not play.

Six AM

I don't know why I have such strong feelings
something is coming to an end.
Maybe I'm misunderstanding my intuition
and something wonderful is about to begin.
I sit here in a flood of emotion,
Six AM and I'm confused and confined
by my lack of explanation
for the answers I'm seeking to find.

Perhaps if I close my eyes and say a prayer
my angels will speak to me
and offer their angelic wisdom
and explain what I feel, but can not see.
Until the moment my prayers are answered
and confusion and confinement ends
I'll sit here feeling something
is about to be over
while hoping something wonderful
is about to begin.

In Defense of a Sunrise

Why do we hail a sunset
and not mention a sunrise?
Is the color so different at evening
from the early morning sky?
Is there a special tone of red
the dawn does not yet know?
Does the sun prefer evening
over the dawn's early glow?
Do clouds conspire with the sunset
so the sunrise can never compete?
No, it's not that a sunset is better,
it's simply at sunrise we're usually asleep.

The Tourists

I can sit here on the sand
and stare out at creation
and I can throw my head back
and see the gulls in flight.
I can close my eyes and the sun
still shines through,
but I'm not alone here in paradise.

I know the tourists have returned again.
I see dedication to relaxing
and their lack of urgency.
I see their slowed pace and movement
as they dig in sand for buried
treasures of the sea.

As I watch them I can't help but think
of how just hours or days before
their voice was heard saying,
"I've not a minute to waste
not one spare second can I afford."

Oh, these are the people who rush
and never seem to have enough time.
The business men and women whose
daily job is to fight over dollars and dimes.

Today I find them in wet baggy swimsuits
and a child's red bucket and shovel in hand.
I'll see them spend two hours examining
a broken shell that is halfway to becoming sand.

Yes, today their big challenge is to dig up
something as rare as a coquina shell.
Do they realize there's a "zillion" more
within each sandy inch and wave that swells?

Now I can sit here and feel the breezes blow
and I can watch the sea grass sway.
But I'm most happy watching the tourists
dig for precious shells that tomorrow
they'll throw away.

The Fairy Tale

The fairy tale is right in front of our eyes.
Before us, but sometimes out of reach.
In the beginning it's hard to determine.
We chance every opportunity
to possibly find love.
We play out each attraction
in hope of securing happiness.
We tend to view things obscurely.
We prefer to see our hopes and wishes
clearer than the truth.
Strengths and weaknesses
are embellished or ignored.

Mistakes are made and overlooked.
Denials lead to second and third chances.
Optimism forges ahead of our common sense.
We follow our hearts, but not our minds.
The fairy tale we are taught in our youth
becomes elusive as we spend our years.
Entitlement to life long love
becomes a fallacy and the dreams
of our youth remains the fairy tale.

Before the Gray

In the white book case
next to my fireplace
in a frame of wood and gold
sits the picture of two old friends
that transcends
to a day when we weren't as old.
One of us wears blue denim
the other a huge grin
and our shoulders hold the others arm.
We sit on a front step
like in the memories we've kept
that remind of our youth forever gone.
Within our eyes we can still see
a trace of the boys we used to be
before wrinkles and gray were blended in.
And the picture in my white bookcase
next to my fireplace
is my favorite of me
and my childhood friend.

The Morning After

The sweet fragrance I recognize as you
has stopped me in my tracks.
I stand in the doorway hoping for another
encounter with the Italian perfume
that reminds me of you.
I'm compelled to enter the room
you used to dress prior to leaving.
I find strands of your hair dotting
my porcelain sink, wet beads from your shower
rolling steadily toward the tile floor
and your still damp towel protrudes
through my fingers as I amorously clutch
it against my cheek.
This gentle fragrance
will always be associated with you.
It brings back memories of moments shared,
evenings spent together and mornings
we went our separate ways.
As I raise my head and face the mirror
it's my image I see.
Your reflection is nowhere to be found
and I am alone, but you are with me
because your scent is here.
These gifts are the remnants from another night,
and in this morning after,
I know you have been here.

The Introduction

Your beauty has captured my eyes.
Your delight has stimulated my imagination.
Yet, I stand here
twenty feet from my possible future.
Glancing over occasionally.
Watching the rhythm in your movement.
Admiring your feminine grace
and amazed at your composure.
I'm intrigued when our eyes connect.
I question your availability.
I realize I can not pass you by.
I wonder who you are?

Your body language indicates
I will be accepted and I move toward you.
My introduction is made with
my hand around your waist.
You smile and extend a warm greeting.
I confirm you are a beautiful woman.
Then, for the first time I hear your voice.
You speak softly, in a self assured tone.
"It's a pleasure to meet you," you quietly say.
And then you turn to introduce me to your companion.
Your eyes dance with truth as you explain,
"I'd like to introduce you to Sandra...
my lover."

Pretending To Love

We pretended to be lovers.
We kissed the way lovers should kiss.
We held each other the way
lovers should hold.
We allowed our hands to touch
the way lovers should touch.
We took the rewards
that should be reserved for lovers.

We felt pulsing hearts,
warm moist bodies
and the release of our intentions.
We pretended to be lovers
and for a few moments
we obliged,
deceived,
abused,
and disrobed
the sanctum of making love.

Falling Asleep

Between reality and dreams
just before I fall asleep
I am closest to you.
When the day has become distant
and worries are forgotten
I find your face again.
As slumber is to sunset,
as harbor is to home
your visits are serene.
You whisper my name,
but where does your voice come from?
As my consciousness fades
it is only important
that you are here, you are with me.

Things I've Lost

Opportunities, memories
and the chance to learn
what I thought I already knew.
Directions to hidden places,
a key to my childhood home
and a picture of
"What was her name?"
Comets across the sky,
satin hair on my pillow
and a cashmere sweater
I loaned out for the night.
A handshake in trust,
a bare tree in an open field
and the innocence that lives prior
to making love for the first time.
A friend that never was,
a streetlight in the snow
and offering my entire life
to one matching soul.
A poem I didn't write,
a song I heard once on the radio
and my high school class ring.
A scribbled autograph,
a tee shirt with a peace sign
and the opportunity to again say,
"I love you".

I've Listened

I've listened to the wind
and recalled how you taught me to describe
wind blown harmonizing voices
singing tranquil lullabies.
You taught me to listen to the sounds
that surround a beating heart.
Now I listen to falling tears
as I search for you alone in the dark.
I've listened to the words
kind friends offer regarding you.
I've listened and accepted
their condolences toward my point of view.
I've listened for your footsteps
upon the hardwood floor.
I've listened for my name
to be called by your voice once more.
Once, as I listened
I heard the wings of angels near.
As I listened, I smiled,
believing you would soon appear.

I've listened to my thoughts
as I ponder my future and fate.
Now, I listen alone in the silence,
since the passing of my love, my mate.

After A While

I still expect to see you
approaching my door.
Sauntering as if time didn't matter.
You were a showcase of vitality.
Defiant and unaware of your destiny.
What would I pay to see you again?

I need to hear your voice.
One more word.
One more thought.

I wish to wrap my arms
around your shoulders.
One more touch.
I would never let you go.

I need one more chance
to disbelieve what is evident.
Allowing me to survive
until the healing begins,
after a while.

After a while,
my memory won't be as vivid as today.
I might forget your childish grin.

After a while,
I may not recall your
jokes that made me laugh,
but I will always recall how I cried,
even after a while.

Certainty is unfamiliar to me.
Today, my faith in tomorrow does not exist.
I will not be able to see you again.
At least not within
the span of my lifetime.
But, I believe
you will be waiting for me in the light
and we shall embrace again
after a while.

Thanks to the very talented Josée Dupont of
Charlesbourg, Quebéc, Canada for the cover design.

Special thanks to...
Janice for inspiration and much more,
my Mother and Father for never ending support,
Alisa, Diane and Neil, Beverly, Dick, Melinda,
Tara, Carol, Dennis, Jessica, and
Baby-cat (even though he left me for the
retired ladies down the street) and all the
unnamed associates who assisted with
this project. Without your proof reading, ideas
and support my second book, Within These Walls,
would not have been possible. Now...
are we ready to go to work on book number three?

Books in print by Robert A. Clay

My Heart's Memory
Published 1997
ISBN 0-9662444-0-0

Within These Walls
Published 2000
ISBN 0-9662444-1-9

*There are split seconds in life many people overlook. Fortunately, Robert Clay recognizes the value of those split seconds and writes beautiful reflective romantic poetry about them. **Within These Walls**, Robert's second book, is filled with split seconds that reveal love, tenderness and a level of sensitivity that few writers come close to understanding. You will find your split seconds in life lingering a little longer when you read the romantic poetry in **Within These Walls**.*

Visit Robert Clay at
www.myheartsmemory.com

ISBN 0-9662444-1-9

9 780966 244410

5 0